JJ Did Tie Buckle

Improve your career by learning, understanding and implementing the USMC Leadership Traits

Perry Hurtt

By Perry Hurtt

Published by Perry L. Hurtt at Smashwords

Copyright 2012 Perry Hurtt

Check out our website at http://www.60KJobs.com for more information and the following books:

$0 to $60K in 90 days - Primer - A free and quick read on the premise of our books.

$0 to $60K in 90 days - Bartender - With no college degree or experience, increase your income to $5K per month after 90 days as a Bartender

$0 to $60K in 90 Days - Unix Administration - With no college degree or experience, increase your income to $5K per month after 90 days as a Unix Administrator

~~

Table of Contents

What to Expect
Who is JJ and what did he do?
Why Marine Corps Leadership?
Meet Ben Franklin (no, he wasn't a Marine)
Time out for some motivation
Justice
Judgment
Decisiveness
Initiative
Dependability
Tact
Integrity
Enthusiasm
Bearing

Unselfishness
Courage
Knowledge
Loyalty
Endurance
Extra Credit
About the Author
Other Works

~

What can you gain from this book? What should you expect?

I learned long ago as an instructor in the Marine Corps that the first and often most important part of any class is to explain to the audience the answer to the question that every one of them is asking themselves: "What's In It For Me", often just abbreviated "WIIFM". I feel it prudent to do the same with this book – to let you know what you can expect.

First, as I've mentioned already and will be apparent throughout this book, I am a Marine. There was a time when I would have said "I'm a former Marine", but the current Commandant of the Marine Corps has issued an order that there are no longer any "former" Marines – if you've served, you are a Marine…with no qualifiers. You might find it odd that I still follow orders although I've been out of the Marine Corps for 11 years now – well, old habits die hard. All of that aside, given the fact that I spent a long time in the Marine Corps and continue to this day to study my beloved Corps, you can expect from me complete (and sometimes brutal) honesty, sound advice, humor, quite a few quotations, more than a few war stories, the occasional swear word…and all of that combined into a book that I know can improve your leadership skills and therefore your ability to be competitive and get ahead in the corporate world. A good bit of research has gone into this book and along the way, I re-acquainted myself with many of the historical heroes of the Marine Corps – you'll have a chance to meet them in the pages that follow. I'll spend some time outlining the amazing feats they performed, how they were recognized, and how their actions fit into the purpose of this book. You'll also learn a bit about ol' Ben Franklin and what an amazing person he was – you'll hear a little from Ralph Waldo

Emerson (my personal favorite) as well as learn about a guy most have never heard of – an amazing man we know simply as Rowan.

So settle in, get a drink, get ready for a fun ride.

~~

Who is JJ and what did he do?

As anybody who has ever dealt with the military knows, there is a fondness of acronyms. One of the key acronyms that are drilled into Marines from day one is the acronym JJDIDTIEBUCKLE (Justice, Judgment, Decisiveness, Initiative, Dependability, Tact, Integrity, Enthusiasm, Bearing, Unselfishness, Courage, Knowledge, Loyalty, and Endurance). This is taught in boot camp and is expected to be remembered and used every day thereafter. From the newest "boot" private to the most senior Enlisted or Officer, every Marine can quote these traits (or at least they *better* be able to) and explain the purpose and importance of each. As a part of promotion boards and inspections, Marines are frequently asked questions about these Leadership Traits – an incorrect answer is not looked upon favorably.

After being lured out of the Marine Corps after almost 17 years of active duty by Corporate America's big money, I came to realize that a healthy dose of JJDIDTIEBUCKLE would be useful in Corporate America.

~~

Why Marine Corps leadership?

Why not Army leadership or Navy leadership? Quite frankly, because it is a foregone conclusion that the leadership taught and practiced by the United States Marine Corps is head and shoulders above the rest of the armed forces – some may deny this or argue about it, but in the end there really is no question. The leadership traits that the Marine Corps is built upon ensure that every Marine, regardless of rank, is capable of leading efficiently and professionally. The other armed forces simply do not teach this throughout the entire rank structure, nor to the level taught and practiced by the Marine Corps. The history of the Marine Corps bears this out. For over 200 years, the Marine Corps has been the expeditionary force in readiness, forward deployed and aggressively responding to crises throughout the world as well as our nation's first line of defense. Marine Corps leadership has been directly responsible for some of history's most dramatic and important events.

Since I "got out", I have worked for a number of managers – most of whom would not be able to hold a candle to the leadership abilities of the freshest Marine Corps NCO, even though these Corporate America managers are often in charge of millions of dollars of resources.

Another distinct difference is the number of people managed. As a Company Gunny or First Sergeant, I was often responsible for hundreds of Marines. As any leadership hierarchy shows, I had key leaders I relied on, but in the end I still had direct contact with hundreds of Marines. In Corporate America, if a manager has more than 10 people working for him/her, it's considered a large organization. At first glance, this seemed downright silly to me (it still does at times) but there is a certain amount of logic. In the Marine Corps, 90% of Marines are highly trained, know their jobs and don't need to be told what to do. In Corporate America, most workers seem to need constant management. Additionally, unlike in the Marine Corps, Corporate America managers directly affect a company's "bottom line" (meaning money). So it is cost effective to the company to have more managers to ensure all workers are actually working. Too many managers and the company ends up paying too much and not getting enough done, resulting in layoffs or other suboptimal conditions so it is a balancing act – lately I'm seeing companies becoming "flatter", with Managers being expected to manage larger teams.

This book is intended to give the reader a competitive edge to ensure a few things:

      Your management skills are the best they can be
      Your team understands you and you understand your team

Your likelihood of being on the chopping block for the next round of layoffs is minimized.

It's important to know them, it's more important to live them.

~

Meet Benjamin Franklin (no, he wasn't a Marine)

So how do you go about actually practicing and learning these traits? It should be a daily effort – something you do consciously and consistently. I harken back to Ben Franklin's process for self-improvement and offer the following as a basis for how this type of effort can be undertaken. Ben was a studious man, and very interested in personal improvement. He spent considerable time creating and then following the below process, to which he eventually credited his many successes.

Ben Franklin identified 12 virtues and described their definitions as such:

Temperance: Eat not to dullness. Drink not to elevation.

Silence: Speak not but what may benefit others or yourself. Avoid trifling conversation.

Order: Let all your things have their places. Let each part of your business have its time.

Resolution: Resolve to perform what you ought. Perform without fail what you resolve.

Frugality: Make no expense but to do good to others or yourself; i.e., waste nothing.

Industry: Lose no time. Be always employed in something useful. Cut off all unnecessary actions.

Sincerity: Use no hurtful deceit. Think innocently and justly; and, if you speak, speak accordingly.

Justice: Wrong none by doing injuries or omitting the benefits that are your duty.

Moderation: Avoid extremes. Forbear resenting injuries so much as you think they deserve.

Cleanliness: Tolerate no uncleanness in body, clothes or habitation.

Tranquility: Be not disturbed at trifles or at accidents common or unavoidable.

Chastity: Rarely use venery [sex] but for health or offspring-never to dullness, weakness, or the injury of your own or another's peace or reputation.

As he showed this list to some of his friends, it was suggested to him that he could also use a healthy dose of *Humility*, of which he typically (in those early days) showed very little. So he added the 13th virtue:

Humility: Imitate Jesus and Socrates

…and there you have Ben's 13 virtues. He wrote these on a sheet of paper in a kind of matrix with seven columns for the days and 13 rows for the virtues – if he had access to Microsoft Excel, he undoubtedly would have used it for this. On a daily basis, he would account for which virtues he succeeded at and which he failed. Rumor has it that he had the most trouble with Humility, going so far as to state "…for even if I could conceive that I had completely overcome pride, I would probably be proud of my humility".

Although he attempted to practice each virtue every day, he realized he needed to focus, and so focused on one virtue primarily for a week, the next week he would move onto the next virtue. With 13 virtues, this allowed him to go through this list 4 times per year, concentrating on one virtue for a week four times each year. He did this for years – it's reported that 50 years later, he could still pull this piece of paper from a pocket and show it to people, such was his determination. Was he successful? Well, we all know he was but few know to what extent. Following is a list of accomplishments by this single man – this man focused on self-improvement – that shows his success:

Scientist – Noted 18th century scientist

Inventor – Invented the stove, the lightning rod, swim fins, watertight bulkheads for ships, an odometer, and others.

Medicine – Founded the 1st US hospital

Banking – Very well known for his thrifty ways

Agriculture – Introduced several crops to US soil

Printing – Known as the "Patron Saint of Printing"

Electrical – Flew the kite, remember?

Insurance – Started the first insurance company (seemed like a good idea at the time)

Heating – Ever heard of the "Franklin Stove"?
Educator – Assisted in the founding of two colleges
Postal – First Postmaster
Library – Started the first circulating library
Journalism – Wrote for several newspapers
Public Safety – Started the first Police Department and the first Fire Department
Religion – Introduced the idea of prayer into Congress
Music – Invented the musical instrument the "glass armonica"
Government – held positions of Clerk, Postmaster, Alderman, Governor and Ambassador
Statesman – help draft the Declaration of Independence
Military – Colonel in the Militia
Masonic – Grand Master of Pennsylvania
Diplomat – Ambassador to England, Minister to France
Businessman – Owned and operated several businesses
Abolitionist – Started Society to Abolish Slavery
Humorist – Considered America's first writer of humor
Forecaster – Published "Poor Richards Almanac"
Cartoonist – Drew first cartoon in American newspaper
Linguist – Studied several languages and designed a phonetic alphabet
Cartographer – Mapped the gulf stream and routes for the post office
Philanthropist – Organized fund raising and contributed to many worthwhile causes

…yeah, I'd say he should be considered a success. Any two or three of the items above would warrant the title of success. That's quite a list!! Maybe this book should be devoted to his process rather than JJDIDTIEBUCKLE? Well the difference here is that his virtues were just that – virtues. Designed to make Ben a better man, his list is a great list to work with to improve your inner self, so to speak. JJDIDTIEBUCKLE are leadership traits, designed to make you a better leader. My point being, the process he used can be used in the same way for JJDIDTIEBUCKLE for those that are so inclined. As mentioned above, today's process would probably involve something like Excel and daily updates on the computer rather than carrying around a piece of paper, but that's fine too – just so long as the effort is undertaken with persistence and sincerity.

We've talked about Ben's virtues; let's now talk about the Marine Corps leadership traits – JJDIDTIEBUCKLE. As a quick rundown, here they are:

Justice
Judgment
Decisiveness
Initiative
Dependability
Tact
Integrity
Enthusiasm
Bearing
Unselfishness
Courage
Knowledge
Loyalty
Endurance

One thing to notice, and again I stress, these are traits to make you a better leader. They are not intended to make you a better husband, wife, brother, daughter, uncle, etc. Although the application of these traits certainly can and will bleed into all areas of your life, they are specifically intended to enhance your leadership qualities. If you end up being a better uncle as well, that's great too.

Marine Corps history is rich with exciting examples of these traits in action. As the Marine's Hymn says, "From the Halls of Montezuma, to the shores of Tripoli", and we should certainly add more recent engagements up to present times to show that these leadership traits are alive and well – the Marine Corps continues to be the strongest, most capable military force in the world due largely to how thoroughly every Marine is instructed to be a leader, regardless of rank.

Why should you emulate the Marine Corps and study these leadership traits? Well, that's a personal question that each will have a different answer for. In the end, there is no doubt that mastering these traits will improve your leadership ability and if that is your goal, then this is a great approach.

~~

Time out for some motivation

Marine Corps Leadership has resulted in a history full of amazing stories. Let's take a quick look at some of the quotes that outline and highlight some of that Marine Corps mystique – and bear in mind these are quotes from highly, important people around the world and often in other services than the Marine Corps:

I have just returned from visiting the Marines at the front, and there is not a finer fighting organization in the world!
General of the Armies Douglas MacArthur; Korea, 21 September 1950

The Marines have landed and the situation is well in hand.
Attributed to Richard Harding Davis (1864-1916)

I come in peace, I didn't bring artillery. But I am pleading with you with tears in my eyes: If you fuck with me, I'll kill you all.
Marine General James Mattis, to Iraqi tribal leaders

The safest place in Korea was right behind a platoon of Marines. Lord, how they could fight!
MGen. Frank E. Lowe, US Army; Korea, 26 January 1952

Marines know how to use their bayonets. Army bayonets may as well be paper-weights.
Navy Times; November 1994

Why in hell can't the Army do it if the Marines can? They are the same kind of men; why can't they be like Marines?
Gen. John J. "Black Jack" Pershing, US Army; 12 February 1918

We have two companies of Marines running rampant all over the northern half of this island, and three Army regiments pinned down in the southwestern corner, doing nothing. What the hell is going on?
Gen. John W. Vessey Jr., US Army, Chairman of the Joint Chiefs of Staff during the assault on Grenada, 1983

They told (us) to open up the Embassy, or "we'll blow you away." And then they looked up and saw the Marines on the roof with these really big guns, and they said in Somali, "Igaralli ahow," which means "Excuse me, I didn't mean it, my mistake".
Karen Aquilar, in the U.S. Embassy; Mogadishu, Somalia, 1991

If I had one more division like this First Marine Division I could win this war.
General of the Armies Douglas McArthur in Korea

I have only two men out of my company and 20 out of some other company. We need support, but it is almost suicide to try to get it here as we are swept by machine gun fire and a constant barrage is on us. I have no one on my left and only a few on my right. I will hold.
1stLt. Clifton B. Cates, USMC in Belleau Wood, 19 July 1918

Do not attack the First Marine Division. Leave the yellowlegs alone. Strike the American Army.
Orders given to Communist troops in the Korean War

There are only two kinds of people that understand Marines: Marines and the enemy. Everyone else has a second-hand opinion.
Gen. William Thornson, U.S. Army

The bended knee is not a tradition of our Corps.
General Alexander A. Vandergrift, USMC to the Senate Naval Affairs Committee, 5 May 1946

Marines I see as two breeds, Rottweilers or Dobermans, because Marines come in two varieties, big and mean, or skinny and mean. They're aggressive on the attack and tenacious on defense. They've got really short hair and they always go for the throat.
Rear Admiral "Jay" R. Stark, US Navy; 10 November 1995

...and my personal two favorites:

The Marines I have seen around the world have the cleanest bodies, the filthiest minds, the highest morale, and the lowest morals of any group of animals I have ever seen. Thank God for the United States Marine Corps!
Eleanor Roosevelt, First Lady of the United States, 1945

Some people spend an entire lifetime wondering if they made a difference in the world. But, the Marines don't have that problem.
Ronald Reagan, President of the United States; 1985

With that kind of praise (and that is indeed a small sampling), can there be any doubt that the methods behind creating Marine Corps leadership is something of value? With this in mind, let's take a look at each of these traits in detail:

~

Justice

Dictionary Definition: The quality of being just or fair

USMC Definition: Justice is defined as the practice of being fair and consistent. A just person gives consideration to each side of a situation and bases rewards or punishments on merit.

Justice is rather the activity of truth, than a virtue in itself. Truth tells us what is due to others, and justice renders that due. Injustice is acting a lie.
Horace Walpole

I tremble for my country when I reflect that God is just; that his justice cannot sleep forever.
Thomas Jefferson

Injustice anywhere is a threat to justice everywhere.
Martin Luther King, Jr.

An ability to prevent and resolve disputes that is based on a "firm but fair" mindset allows Marines to function efficiently in the chaotic conditions that combat is known for. Decisions made at the highest and lowest ranks that are done so impartially, consistently and justly ensures unit cohesion and effectiveness.

It's not hard to imagine how and why Justice is a critical leadership trait – the ability to always be "firm, fair and consistent" when dealing with other Marines or with co-workers will lead to a more effective working environment.

Looking through the annals of history, you won't find anybody awarded the Medal of Honor for a strong sense of Justice – it's not something that normally results in any kind of Medal or award. But, there is a great example to be observed regarding how Lt. John R. Fox (US Army) was posthumously awarded the Medal of Honor for his actions in World War II while serving in Italy. To allow his unit to withdraw from a lopsided firefight against battle hardened Nazis, Lt. Fox called in an artillery strike on his own location. The artillery strike was accurate, and more than 100 Nazi soldiers were killed, as was Lt. Fox and five other American soldiers (one other American Soldier was wounded, but survived) – but the action was a success and enabled the rest of the unit to withdraw and regroup. At the time, this group of men were not given due notice however, because they were all black. No medals, no mentions of bravery, no honors. It wasn't until a half century later that these men and their actions were officially recognized and all seven were awarded the Medal of Honor – six of them posthumously. The eventual recognition of their ultimate sacrifice is a solid example of Justice in action and reflects the new mindset of Americans as to the importance of recognizing everybody's contributions, regardless of race.

In the corporate world, an employee's enthusiasm for work as well as loyalty rely heavily on three things – pay, perks and recognition. All three of these are directly related to Justice in that they should be awarded fairly based on competence and performance, rather than personal preferences or "who knows who". In an environment where certain employees consistently receive preferential treatment due to favoritism on the part of the managers, morale will suffer greatly.

Pay – in the military, everybody knows what everybody else makes so this is absolutely not an issue. This information is published yearly and is available to every military member (and civilians). This was a difficult thing for me to comprehend in my transition to the military, the fact that pay was not discussed among employees. In a sense of fairness, and therefore Justice, workers in civilian companies are paid based on how well they negotiate their salary/wage before they are hired, and after that depending on the size of their raises. For Management, ensuring proper compensation for the work being done is critical – it's not difficult for anybody to see how the compare industry wide for the work being done and if there is a perception of being underpaid then the job hunt begins. Keep the pay competitive to ensure your work force isn't spending half their time job hunting.

Perks – these come in many flavors. My favorite is cash. Most companies have several different systems in place to reward things like innovation, quota attainment, longevity, etc, etc. Some award gifts, some award money – guess which is the favorite? Regardless of what the method of reward is, they must be given fairly. One person on a team of four that receives five $100 American Express gift certificates for "job well done" while the other four workers receive none is either extreme favoritism or a case of a team with four very bad employees. Usually – sadly to say – it's the former. Ensure team members receive perks fairly.

Recognition – it's been said that public recognition is better than either pay or perks. Most people, even if they won't admit it, truly love to hear their names and accomplishments shared by their leaders. In this world of extreme competition, public recognition is also a signal that the team has a real star in it's midst (a bonus for the team leader for developing such a star) as well as a feather in the cap for the person so recognized.

Action Items:
>   Take a hard look at yourself to determine if you have any prejudices towards others. Many people do and don't realize it. Old, skinny, fat, poor, ethnic difference, religious differences, etc, etc – any of these can be a basis for unfair actions
>
>   Ensure there is a sound policy for rewards and punishments and that you follow these policies strictly and impersonally. If a policy does not exist or is lacking, take the lead on creating or improving it. Showing favoritism will undermine your perceived (or actual) sense of justice and therefore undermine your leadership abilities.
>
>   Don't get caught in the trap of only serving praise or only serving punishment – a strong sense of justice should allow you to do both equally and consistently.

~~

Judgment

Dictionary Definition: The act of judging or assessing a person or situation or event

USMC Definition: Judgment is your ability to think about things clearly, calmly, and in an orderly fashion so that you can make good decisions.

At twenty years of age the will reigns; at thirty, the wit; and at forty, the judgment.
Benjamin Franklin

Good judgment comes from experience. Experience comes from bad judgment
Oscar Wilde

I ask you to judge me by the enemies I have made
Franklin D. Roosevelt

Since judgment goes hand in hand with experience, younger Marines are always in "learning mode" to gain wisdom as they gain experience. The best laid plan will fail if based on poor judgment, and Marines don't fail. Every Marine is afforded many opportunities to either gain experience or learn from other's experiences as they progress through the ranks.

Love him or hate him, you have to admire his judgment in his selection of a VP. Barack Obama chose Joe Biden based on how Biden matched up against the requirements of the office, rather than how many votes he thought Biden would bring in. On the other side of the ticket was an obvious (and laughable) ploy to get votes when McCain named Sarah Palin as his running mate. If nothing else, this provided the late night comedians with ample material and kept us laughing for many months. In the end, though, Americans saw through this ploy and nobody argues it was bad judgment on the McCain party. I'm not trying to get too far into the political arena on this subject, but time has shown that Biden was an effective VP – further substantiating Obama's judgment in selecting him.

Militarily speaking…and of course with a strong USMC flavor, nobody displayed better judgment under fire then Lewis B. Puller, or as every Marine knows of him, Chesty Puller. A distant cousin of Army General George Patton, Chesty was the recipient of 5 Navy Cross's, the Distinguished Service Cross, the Silver Star, the Purple Heart, the Bronze Star with Valor, 2 Legions of Merit with Valor, and a host of other awards and commendations; this is the stuff of legends regarding combat and Marine Corps history. He could easily be highlighted in any of the 14 leadership traits, but I chose "judgment" simply because most of the others were so obvious. "Courage"? Obviously he had that in spades. "Dependability"? Check. Etc, etc, so I wanted to talk about his judgment.

The stories of how he earned his medals are varied and exciting, but let's talk about how he earned his fourth Navy Cross, as this is a great example of solid judgment in the most trying of times.

In the battle at Cape Gloucester, New Britain during World War II, given temporary command of 3rd 'Battalion, 7th Marines, he also assumed command of 3rd Battalion, 5th Marines when their Commanding Office and the Executive Officer were both wounded and unable to command. Commanding both Battalions, Chesty was able to effectively reorganize the units and move towards their objective. While holding key terrain along a fire swept ridge, Chesty moved from company to company, redirecting fire as needed, reorganizing units to maintain critical positions, all the while being exposed to enemy rifle, machine-gun and mortar fire. On this day, as on many others, Chesty displayed unparalleled courage and determination – he also displayed uncanny judgment in his management of the many companies under his control against a well-entrenched and enemy. His judgment saved many lives in that battle and many others and has served as an example for Marines to follow forever.

Exercising sound judgment in a corporate setting is a bit different – you're usually not called upon to ensure your machine guns have effective fields of fire. However, you are tasked with making decisions, or enabling your teams to make decisions – sometimes without all of the facts. This comes into play for both team members as well as managers.

As a team member, there will be times that it is necessary to judge whether you have the experience and knowledge to make a decision or if that decision should be passed to your manager. As a Manager, you need to be able to judge which of your team members are capable of making the big decisions. This is a good example of the difference between Judgment and Decisiveness – an often asked question. As a Manager you must have the Judgment to be able to tell which of your team members can make the decisions. As a team member, you must have the Judgment to determine if you are the right person to make a critical decision.

Another critical example of Judgment for Managers is evaluating your team members to determine who the "A" players are and who aren't. The "A" players, of course, are the people you know you can rely on in any situation. Hopefully there's at least one, maybe two on your team. If your entire team is made up of true "A" players, then you're hogging all the talent and you should share.

Action Items:
> When possible, get all the facts before rendering judgment. When all of the facts are not available, make your judgment calls carefully
>
> Exercise a high degree of common sense when dealing with situations that require good judgment. Many times, what is considered a "good judgment call" is, in reality, a healthy dose of common sense.
>
> Evaluate yourself and your team – use good Judgment to ascertain who among your team members the "A" players are. Deploy these team members to gain the most of their skills. The rest of your team members should be evaluated for their ability to become the next "A" player and then treated as such. Sometimes, you just have to separate the wheat from the chaff.

~

Decisiveness

Dictionary Definition: The trait of resoluteness as evidenced by firmness of character or purpose

USMC Definition: Ability to make decisions promptly and to announce them in clear, forceful manner

Decisiveness is a characteristic of high-performing men and women. Almost any decision is better than no decision at all.
Brian Tracy

The way to develop decisiveness is to start right where you are, with the very next question you face.
Napoleon Hill

It's better to be boldly decisive and risk being wrong than to agonize at length and be right too late.
Marilyn Moats Kennedy

Believing that the worst decision is to not make a decision at all, Marines are taught throughout their entire time in the Marine Corps to be decisive. Training in decision making during peace time greatly enhances a Marine's decision making ability during the heat of battle.

The story of William Earl Barber, a Marine Corps Captain during the Korean War, is a defining example of decisiveness under extreme pressure. Only 220 men remained under his command and he faced 1,400 communist Chinese soldiers in the frigid Chosin Resevior. With a broken leg and having received orders to leave his position, he refused as he believed such an action would leave another 8,000 Marines cut off and trapped – he refused his orders. After six days of fighting, the Chinese had suffered over 1,000 casualties – Captain Barber had only 82 of his men in walking condition, but his decision to reject the orders and stand fast was proven to be the right move – he was later awarded the Congressional Medal of Honor for his decisions and his actions.

The Marine Corps leadership is based on a concept of "Commander's Intent", which means that Marines at the unit level must understand the thought process and the intent of the leaders above them. This gives the lower level leaders the ability to make decisions as circumstances change but also gives them a basis for making those decisions. Some lateral flexibility is built into this process so lower level units can adapt to changing circumstances while still staying on course with the primary mission. This is not done in a vacuum as intensive training prior to combat ensures all Marines understand this concept and have the ability to act in accordance.

As Sun Tzu said, "…when you see the correct course, act. Do not wait for orders".

"Commander's Intent" can easily be envisioned in a corporate setting. If you are in Sales, your Regional Sales Manager's intent is pretty obvious – make quota. In this respect, are you given the ability to make decisions that support that intent or are you hamstrung by corporate policies that inhibit this? Are you able to take immediate and thorough steps to resolve a customer complaint or is there a bureaucratic process to slow you down? Sales is a fairly easy example, but what if you're in a different position where the distinction is not quite so clear? The underlying question remains the same – have you been given the ability to make decisions in the best interest of the company to overcome objections or to fix customer complaints? If not, then your role probably does not enable you to support the "Commander's Intent".

Action Items:

Work on making quick decisions and then sticking with those decisions as long as they are deemed to be sound. Listen to other's input and advice, then do your own research and give it your own consideration and then make the decision. This can sound like a lengthy process but in reality sometimes it has to take place in the blink of an eye. Regardless, make the decision!

Look back over the past few key decisions you've made and determine how you arrived at that decision. Would you consider that decision the correct course of action now, with hindsight to aid you? Did you have all the facts when you made the decision? Did anybody oppose the decision? Why?

Determine the answer to the Commanders Intent questions posed earlier. If your position does not support this, resolve to talk to your manager about this.

~~

Initiative

Dictionary Definition: Serving to set in motion

USMC Definition: Taking action in the absence of orders

During my service in the United States Congress, I took the initiative in creating the Internet.
Al Gore

I've always had confidence. It came because I have lots of initiative. I wanted to make something of myself.
Eddie Murphy

Initiative is doing the right thing without being told.
Victor Hugo

Always looking for ways to improve the situation at hand, no Marine waits to be told what to do. A strong sense of initiative enables every Marine to be a leader, whether at home or on in combat.

Leonard Foster, a Marine Corps Private First Class (PFC), during combat in World War II in Guam, received the Congressional Medal of Honor for his actions when his patrol came under fire from 2 machine guns at a range of about 15 yards. While others remained pinned down,

PFC Foster, of his own initiative, moved out of the gulley his platoon was trapped in and advanced towards the machines guns – getting wounded several times in the process. He was able to kill 5 Japanese soldiers and wounded another, effectively taking out the enemy machine gun nests on his own. He later died of the wounds he received during this action.

In a corporate setting, initiative will separate the leaders from the followers. Leaders have high degrees of initiative – seeing what needs to be done and getting it done without needing to be told. A good way to look at this in your job is to picture yourself as the owner of the company – if you owned the company and saw something that needed to be done, would you do it? Of course you would – it would benefit your company! Do this enough times, and eventually the company (or another) will be yours for the taking.

Many workers may feel they don't have the authority to do something when they see it needs to be done. Rest easy here – it's far better to do it then to not. If you screw it up, your manager will still (or at least should) recognize your initiative in at least attempting it.

It's worthwhile to note that many of the Leadership Traits you are reading about are paralleled in civilian communities but are often referred to by different names. In Stephen Covey's landmark book The Seven Habits of Highly Effective People", his first habit is "Be Proactive"…which means exactly the same as the Marine Corps Leadership trait of "Initiative".

Action Items
- Volunteer. In the military, a common piece of advice is to never volunteer for anything. At times, that's pretty good advice unless you're fond of burying lockers in the desert or standing gear watch in the freezing cold. However, in most cases volunteering gives you the opportunity to exercise your initiative. Often, a job volunteered for is a blank slate upon which you can paint your own story – showing your creativity, resourcefulness and your initiative. So volunteer, and then do the best job possible.

- Take a good look around and see what can be improved – and then improve it. Even if nobody is watching, even if nobody else will know, do it anyway. As this becomes a habit, it will show through in many other ways to the point where others will take notice.

- Call your friends and family. Odd, I know…but taking the initiative to reach out to people you don't talk to enough pays off in many wonderful ways. Reconnect to people you haven't talked to in a long time and see where that takes you.

~~

Dependability

Dictionary Definition: The trait of being dependable or reliable

USMC Definition: Dependability - The certainty of proper performance of duty.

> *Ability without dependability is worthless*
> Unknown

Those guys are Ferraris; I'm an F-150. They go in every 3,000 miles, but I go 100,000 before you start changing the oil. The durability and dependability, that's where my benefits come in.
Jerome Bettis

Dependability is that quality of sureness which makes folks know that the task assigned will be accomplished, that the promise made will be kept, a golden quality
Clarissa Beesley

Dependability is a fundamental virtue, without which all of the nobler and finer qualities of character are greatly discounted, and without it the complicated society in which we live could not be maintained.
Bryant S. Hinckley

There can be no doubt that a Marine can always be counted on – this is something that is bred into Marines from the first day of boot camp and continues forever. Marines are known as problem solvers, not excuse makers – if it can be done, a Marine will get it done. Often – when most think it can't be done, a Marine will still get it done.

When the topic of Dependability comes up, I'm always reminded of a conversation I had with a boss a while ago when I was contemplating looking for another job. My position had grown a bit stale, I thought there was more money to be had elsewhere, and quite frankly I was just ready for a change. My manager was also a close friend, so I felt comfortable being very up front with him and tell him what I was considering. It was a long conversation, a lot of emotion, a lot of bargaining and promises. But one thing he said that has stuck with me was that he needed to know if I was somebody he could depend on – would I be there for him. Could he put me in the critical path of a project and know that I would stay the course and finish it? My answer at the time was "no, because I'll be looking elsewhere for work". This lead to more bargaining and some eventual promises of pay raises and additional perks that eventually led me to stay at the job. But, his questions to me that day: "Can I depend on you? Can I put you in the critical path of a project?" have always stuck with me as key questions because really – shouldn't this be a question for every employee?

Dependability is not just being there when the boss needs you, it's also being there when anybody needs you, it's putting in the required effort (and then some) required to get the job done, it's putting in a full day's effort every day.

On the next few pages, I've included the text of an essay that was written over 100 years ago – it's titled "A Message to Garcia". In it, a man named Rowan is portrayed as the ultimately dependable person – somebody you want on your team.

A Message To Garcia – Elbert Hubbard

In all this Cuban business there is one man stands out on the horizon of my memory like Mars at perihelion.

When war broke out between Spain & the United States, it was very necessary to communicate quickly with the leader of the Insurgents. Garcia was somewhere in the mountain vastness of Cuba- no one knew where. No mail nor telegraph message could reach him. The President must secure his cooperation, and quickly.

What to do!

Some one said to the President, "There's a fellow by the name of Rowan will find Garcia for you, if anybody can."

Rowan was sent for and given a letter to be delivered to Garcia. How "the fellow by the name of Rowan" took the letter, sealed it up in an oil-skin pouch, strapped it over his heart, in four days landed by night off the coast of Cuba from an open boat, disappeared into the jungle, & in three weeks came out on the other side of the Island, having traversed a hostile country on foot, and delivered his letter to Garcia, are things I have no special desire now to tell in detail. The point I wish to make is this: McKinley gave Rowan a letter to be delivered to Garcia; Rowan took the letter and did not ask, "Where is he at?"

By the Eternal! there is a man whose form should be cast in deathless bronze and the statue placed in every college of the land. It is not book-learning young men need, nor instruction about this and that, but a stiffening of the vertebrae which will cause them to be loyal to a trust, to act promptly, concentrate their energies: do the thing- "Carry a message to Garcia!"

General Garcia is dead now, but there are other Garcias. No man, who has endeavored to carry out an enterprise where many hands were needed, but has been well nigh appalled at times by the imbecility of the average man- the inability or unwillingness to concentrate on a thing and do it.
Slip-shod assistance, foolish inattention, dowdy indifference, & half-hearted work seem the rule; and no man succeeds, unless by hook or crook, or threat, he forces or bribes other men to assist him; or mayhap, God in His goodness performs a miracle, & sends him an Angel of Light for an assistant.

You, reader, put this matter to a test: You are sitting now in your office- six clerks are within call. Summon any one and make this request: "Please look in the encyclopedia and make a brief memorandum for me concerning the life of Correggio."

Will the clerk quietly say, "Yes, sir," and go do the task? On your life, he will not. He will look at you out of a fishy eye and ask one or more of the following questions:

Who was he?
Which encyclopedia?
Where is the encyclopedia?
Was I hired for that?
Don't you mean Bismarck?
What's the matter with Charlie doing it?
Is he dead?
Is there any hurry?
Shan't I bring you the book and let you look it up yourself? What do you want to know for?

And I will lay you ten to one that after you have answered the questions, and explained how to find the information, and why you want it, the clerk will go off and get one of the other clerks to help him try to find Garcia- and then come back and tell you there is no such man. Of course I may lose my bet, but according to the Law of Average, I will not.

Now if you are wise you will not bother to explain to your "assistant" that Correggio is indexed under the C's, not in the K's, but you will smile sweetly and say, "Never mind," and go look it up yourself. And this incapacity for independent action, this moral stupidity, this infirmity of the will, this unwillingness to cheerfully catch hold and lift, are the things that put pure Socialism so far into the future. If men will not act for themselves, what will they do when the benefit of their effort is for all?
A first-mate with knotted club seems necessary; and the dread of getting "the bounce" Saturday night, holds many a worker to his place. Advertise for a stenographer, and nine out of ten who apply, can neither spell nor punctuate- and do not think it necessary to.

Can such a one write a letter to Garcia?

"You see that bookkeeper," said the foreman to me in a large factory.

"Yes, what about him?"

"Well he's a fine accountant, but if I'd send him up town on an errand, he might accomplish the errand all right, and on the other hand, might stop at four saloons on the way, and when he got to Main Street, would forget what he had been sent for."

Can such a man be entrusted to carry a message to Garcia?

We have recently been hearing much maudlin sympathy expressed for the "downtrodden denizen of the sweat-shop" and the "homeless wanderer searching for honest employment," & with it all often go many hard words for the men in power.

Nothing is said about the employer who grows old before his time in a vain attempt to get frowsy ne'er-do-wells to do intelligent work; and his long patient striving with "help" that does nothing but loaf when his back is turned. In every store and factory there is a constant weeding-out process going on. The employer is constantly sending away "help" that have shown their incapacity to further the interests of the business, and others are being taken on. No matter how good times are, this sorting continues, only if times are hard and work is scarce, the sorting is done finer- but out and forever out, the incompetent and unworthy go. It is the survival of the fittest. Self-interest prompts every employer to keep the best- those who can carry a message to Garcia.

I know one man of really brilliant parts who has not the ability to manage a business of his own, and yet who is absolutely worthless to any one else, because he carries with him constantly the insane suspicion that his employer is oppressing, or intending to oppress him. He cannot give orders; and he will not receive them. Should a message be given him to take to Garcia, his answer would probably be, "Take it yourself."
Tonight this man walks the streets looking for work, the wind whistling through his threadbare coat. No one who knows him dare employ him, for he is a regular firebrand of discontent. He is impervious to reason, and the only thing that can impress him is the toe of a thick-soled No. Nine boot.

Of course I know that one so morally deformed is no less to be pitied than a physical cripple; but in our pitying, let us drop a tear, too, for the men who are striving to carry on a great enterprise, whose working hours are not limited by the whistle, and whose hair is fast turning white through the struggle to hold in line dowdy indifference, slip-shod imbecility, and the heartless ingratitude, which, but for their enterprise, would be both hungry & homeless.

Have I put the matter too strongly? Possibly I have; but when all the world has gone a-slumming I wish to speak a word of sympathy for the man who succeeds-the man who, against great odds has directed the efforts of others, and having succeeded, finds there's nothing in it: nothing but bare board and clothes. I have carried a dinner pail & worked for day's wages, and I have also been an employer of labor, and I know there is something to be said on both sides. There is no excellence, per se, in poverty; rags are no recommendation; & all employers are not rapacious and high-handed, any more than all poor men are virtuous. My heart goes out to the man who does his work when the "boss" is away, as well as when he is at home. And the man who, when given a letter for Garcia, quietly take the missive, without asking any idiotic questions, and with no lurking intention of chucking it into the nearest sewer, or of doing aught else but deliver it, never gets "laid off," nor has to go on a strike for higher wages.

Civilization is one long anxious search for just such individuals. Anything such a man asks shall be granted; his kind is so rare that no employer can afford to let him go. He is wanted in every city, town and village-in every office, shop, store and factory.

The world cries out for such: he is needed, & needed badly-the man who can carry a message to Garcia.

Action Items:

Look over the past couple of weeks or month and identify where you may have dropped ball when others were depending on you. Why did that happen? Were external factors part of the cause? Is there anything you could/should have done differently? Did it just not seem important at the time? Resolve to accomplish what you agree to without fail, without excuses. If external factors come into play, it's your responsibility to account for those factors to ensure they do not negatively impact an outcome to which you have committed.

As above, look over the past couple of weeks or months but this time look for instances where you believe went "above and beyond" expectations to fulfill a commitment or an expectation. Why were you able to perform at that level – was it an easy task? What is critical? Was it enjoyable? Learn from these successful instances so you can be better prepared for the next one that comes along.

In the future, be very careful what you agree to – remember that your happiness, your reputation and quite likely your livelihood depends on this. If the effort consists of portions that are out of your control, ensure everybody realizes this. If the effort is something you know you will not enjoy, and therefore procrastinate on, be prepared for this and be resolute in your efforts.

Emulate Rowan

~~

Tact

Dictionary Definition: Consideration in dealing with others and avoiding giving offence

USMC Definition: The ability to deal with others without creating offense

Tact is the ability to describe others as they see themselves.
Abraham Lincoln

Tact is the art of making a point without making an enemy.
Isaac Newton

"Tact is the art of making guests feel at home when that is really where you wish they were.
Anonymous

How something is said or portrayed is often more important than the act itself. Marines are taught to find a way to deal with others in the most appropriate manner so that everybody works together as a team to achieve a common goal. This is critical as much when working with other Marines as it is when working with locals in a remote land.

A great example of Tact in action is the professional men and women that make up the Military Police. Let me say first, I understand that there are examples of unprofessionalism in this area, as in any other. I'm talking about the ones who do their jobs professionally – these guys are the epitome of "Tact". Why? Well, on a daily basis their jobs require them to interact with military members that are higher ranking then they are – sometimes quite a bit higher. Imagine the situation when a young Corporal needs to pull over a higher rank (a Major, for example) for something like speeding. With Tact, the Corporal can handle the situation without offending the Major while at the same time doing his job professionally. A healthy dose of Bear is helpful here as well – and not just on the part of the Corporal but the Major as well. It's not hard to imagine the Major using his rank to influence the Corporal's action – likewise it's not difficult to imagine the Corporal going on a bit of a power trip and abusing his role as Military Police. However, with Tact in place, backed by a high degree of Bearing and professionalism, neither of these occurrences are likely to happen.

In a corporate setting, consider the situation when you know more than your manager. Maybe your manager has said something that is incorrect. Maybe it's not your manager...maybe it's the regional manager or even higher up the food chain. The point is, consider yourself in the situation where you need to provide some kind of correction against what your boss has publicly stated – how do you do it.

Do you blurt it out in front of everybody? No...bad idea. You make your boss look bad – never a good idea.

Do you simply cover up his mistake by taking over the conversation and inserting the accurate information in as appropriate? Maybe...if that will work. Taking over the conversation will depend a good deal on the subject being discussed and the level of the participants. So tread carefully here

Do you pull him aside later and explain your understanding so he can then make the correction on his own? This would probably be the 'best' course of action in most cases.

Action items:
>Most people fall into either acting too tactfully or not acting tactfully enough. If you are too tactful, your results can suffer as you may not come right out and ask or demand for something to be done. If you are not tactful enough, you may be getting things done but at the expense of your image and ultimate usefulness as nobody wants to deal with a tactless person in the long term. Take the time to perform a good self-analysis to identify where you fit and make a commitment to alter how you act in situations that require tact.
>
>The next time you are asked "what do you want for dinner" or "where do you want to go" or "what do you want to do", tactfully explain what you would like to do rather than the usual answer of "I don't care, whatever you want".
>
>Consider the next meeting you are to attend. It's usually pretty easy to envision what types of items will be discussed and come up with a predictable set of questions and answers that will be thrown around. Find one item you are passionate about and prepare to defend your position tactfully. Being prepared, having the facts at hand, and having run through it in your mind a few times will be of immense value and enable you to go through with it with a clear head.

～

Integrity

Dictionary Definition: Moral soundness

USMC Definition: Uprightness of character and soundness of moral principles; includes the qualities of truthfulness and honesty

Nothing is at last sacred but the integrity of your own mind.
Ralph Waldo Emerson

Real integrity is doing the right thing, knowing that nobody's going to know whether you did it or not.
Oprah Winfrey

Integrity has no need of rules.
Albert Camus

Marines consider Integrity to be the first layer to be built, upon which all other character traits are based – it is the cornerstone of character. Without Integrity, there is no trust – without the trust of your fellow Marines, there can be no successful mission. To gain integrity, Marines are taught to act with honor at all times, regardless of whether anybody else is there to see.

Integrity is not just a personal issue – it can and should be (must be) an organizationally wide trait as well. A few years ago, a Marine Pilot crashed his jet into a San Diego neighborhood during a training mission, killing four people. Most corporations and certainly most Government entities would do everything in their power to sidestep blame in an occurrence such as this, but the Marine Corps initiated an investigation of it's own and ultimately took full responsibility in the eyes of the public. Although tragic, this served as a very good example of the Marine Corps practicing what it preaches – being responsible for your actions and doing what is right no matter what the cost.

An interesting example of integrity in action is the most recent Medal of Honor Recipient for the Marine Corps, Sgt Dakota Meyers. There was a lot of discussion as to whether it was deserved or not – and truthfully Sgt Meyers himself is probably the only one that can answer that. I'm not trying to sort that out. What happened after he left the Marine Corps is interesting though. He went to work for a company that made and sold thermal imaging devices to assist in finding explosive devices. He eventually ended up on a team that was responsible for selling these devices to Pakistan. He voiced his concern about selling the best technology on the market to a country known for having dealings with enemy countries as well as terrorist organizations and was belittled. The company actually reported him as being mentally unstable and claimed drinking issues – an apparent attempt to discredit so the sales of the Thermal Imaging devices could proceed. Sgt Meyers' actions during this time showed great integrity.

So what about integrity in the civilian workplace? The same rules apply – do what needs to be done when you know it needs to be done to the level it needs to be done to the best of your ability. Don't compromise

Action Items:
A critical part of the gaining and maintaining integrity is doing the "right" thing whether anybody is watching or not. Given this, think about the last couple of weeks (or further if you can) and identify times when you may have done something that weakened or strengthened your integrity. If you did something that weakened it, why did you do it? Why didn't you do the "right" thing?

Put yourself on notice that you will maintain the highest degree of integrity. I envision a person acting as though they feel like their mother, their lawyer and their religious leader are always watching them. So the next time you're faced with what could be a difficult situation, ask yourself what you would do if your mother, lawyer and priest were standing there with you…and then do it.

Enforce a high level of integrity from those around you – your family, friends and co-workers. Do this by leading by example, acting with a high degree of integrity and slowly start pointing out times when others are not. This might be painful at first and may cause some friction – but if you consider the alternative it should be an effort that is well worth the time.

~~

Enthusiasm

Dictionary Definition: A lively interest

USMC Definition: The display of sincere interest and exuberance in the performance of duty

A man can succeed at almost anything for which he has unlimited enthusiasm.
Charles Schwab

Enthusiasm glows, radiates, permeates and immediately captures everyone's interest.
Paul J. Meyer

Enthusiasm is the mother of effort, and without it nothing great was ever achieved.
Ralph Waldo Emerson

Marines are taught that anything worth doing is worth doing well. Understanding that Enthusiasm is a critical part of doing something well, motivation for any effort by Marines is contagious, creating enthusiasm by all participants, thereby increasing the likelihood of a successful outcome.

Enthusiasm has been described as one of the most powerful engines of success. The urge to do something and do it well, putting all your possible energies and thoughts into it to make sure the outcome is the best it can be, and doing so with the best possible mindset is a sure fire recipe for success. Team interactions benefit tremendously from enthusiasm as it is truly contagious.

Enthusiasm is one of those traits that you can "fake it until you make it" in many instances. Bearing in mind the importance of enthusiasm to actually accomplish anything of value, becoming enthusiastic about your undertaking is important. Dale Carnegie urges us to act enthusiastic until we become enthusiastic – acting leads to feeling.

A perfect example of Enthusiasm would be Winston Churchill – one of his recognized chief attributes was that he always demonstrated enthusiasm, determination and optimism. If you look at the timeframe of which Winston Churchill controlled the military might of the British armed forces, it's easy to understand the need for somebody with unbridled enthusiasm and determination to be a driving force. Churchill fully understood the danger of having a defeatist attitude or poor morale, so he continuously set the example – one of his own sayings was "We must KBO", which meant "Keep Buggering On". To ensure morale and optimism was high during some of the dreariest days in history, Winston Churchill just "buggering on".

Action Items:
    They say Enthusiasm is contagious (I even said it above). Test that theory. Find something you are enthusiastic about and talk it over with people who know you – see if you can get them excited. After that, try it on people you don't know very well…maybe even complete strangers if the setting is appropriate.

    The next time you are faced with a task you aren't enthusiastic about, find a reason for enthusiasm anyway – it's not hard to do. Cleaning out the little box and a little bummed about that? Think of how much nicer the house will smell afterwards and how grateful your wife or kids will be.

    Take stock of the truly memorable achievements in your life and work to identify how enthusiastic you were about them – and what caused that enthusiasm. If you can find the root of what causes your enthusiasm, it helps you to draw on this amazing power at will.

〜

Bearing

Dictionary Definition: Dignified manner or conduct

USMC Definition: Creating a favorable impression in carriage, appearance and personal conduct at all times.

Arnold Schwarzenegger, I don't know if you'd call him a great actor, but he's amazing in terms of his presence [bearing], and he is interesting enough that you want to watch him.
F. Murray Abraham

An actor is totally vulnerable. His total personality is exposed to critical judgment - his intellect, his bearing, his diction, his whole appearance. In short, his ego.
Alec Guinness

I think Ronald Reagan was one of the great presidents, period, not just recently. I thought he had the demeanor. I thought he had the bearing. I thought he had the thought process.
Donald Trump

Marines are known for their impeccable uniforms, their ram-rod straight posture, confidence and a no nonsense approach. Marines are taught that they are ambassadors for the United States and the Marine Corps and they understand the importance of this role, exemplifying the standards set forth in everything they do. A Marine's bearing is often the first thing noticed.

Bearing is a way of carrying yourself – a way of presenting yourself as a person that commands and deserves respect. Each discrepancy of your appearance and manner take a chunk away from your Bearing – eventually to the point where you simply have none. We've all seen people from opposite ends of the spectrum – either the person who walks into a room and doesn't have to say a word yet everybody senses that here is a person to be reckoned with – a true force. Or, the opposite person, slinking around trying their best to not be noticed.

Ralph Waldo Emerson, in his essay on Character: "Half his strength, he put not forth. His victories are by demonstration of superiority, and not by crossing of bayonets. He conquers because his arrival alters the face of affairs". This is a good accounting of one's Bearing – a latent, maybe completely unrecognizable force of a person – yet it is there and you feel it.

In Military life, Bearing is important in many ways. It is a measure of how competently a Marine acts under pressure – in this respect you could think of it as poise. Keeping a cool head and "not losing your bearing" is something that is taught and expected of every Marine regardless of rank. Two perfect examples of Marines with bearing are Recruiters and Drill Instructors – two of the most prominently visible positions held by Marines. You also see this displayed when you see the President walking the grounds and you see Marines in the background – or when the President boards his helicopter and the young Jarhead snaps a perfect salute…examples of Marines with perfect Bearing.

In civilian life, Bearing is important as well. When things begin to go wrong for whatever reason, a manager or leader with strong Bearing will remain calm and think through the situation – showing neither nervousness nor panic to his teams. He may be feeling panic on the inside, but understands that to show this to his teams would be counterproductive.

We've all see the guy or lady that walks into a room and other people instantly know that this person is one to be reckoned with – a person of strong presence, healthy confidence, knowledge and no fear of anything or anybody else in the room. This person doesn't have to be the senior person in the room either – it can be one of the lower ranking people but there is a sense about this person that they will go on to do great things. When you feel this, you are sensing the other person's strong sense of Bearing.

Action Items:

Take extra care with the clothes you wear on any given day. "Clothes don't make the man", as they say, but when you go the extra mile and ensure your clothes are clean and neatly pressed, your shoes are shined, and you have a clean shave – you just *feel* better.

An important part of having good Bearing is confidence. If your confidence is lacking, so is your bearing. Confidence is gained by knowledge and experience – so the point here is to know what you're doing. Don't walk into a meeting unprepared. Have more knowledge than those around you and share gracefully.

If you don't routinely wear a suit, try it for a day or two and see how it feels. This, of course, depends on what you do for a living. If you're changing the oil in cars all day, this probably doesn't apply to you quite so much…but there's nothing stopping you from putting that suit on for a night on the town!

__*

Unselfishness

Dictionary Definition: The quality of not putting yourself first but being willing to give your time or money or effort etc. for others

USMC Definition: Avoidance of providing for one's own comfort and personal advancement at the expense of others

Confidence... thrives on honesty, on honor, on the sacredness of obligations, on faithful protection and on unselfish performance. Without them it cannot live.
Franklin D. Roosevelt

To live a pure unselfish life, one must count nothing as one's own in the midst of abundance.
Buddha

One great, strong unselfish could in every community could actually redeem the world
Elbert Hubbard

Marines are, by nature, an unselfish group – who else would sign up for this kind of life with little pay. Throughout time in the Marine Corps, Marines are taught a "team before self" mentality that serves well in combat and on the home front.

Unselfishness is the act, or maybe the mindset and the act, of putting the consideration others before yourself. This trait is one in which most leaders or managers will claim the utmost possession and yet, in reality, finding a truly unselfish leader is quite rare. In today's highly competitive market, everybody is scratching to make the best name possible for themselves and if that means taking credit for another's work or effort, so be it. I've seen countless managers in Corporate America that fall into this trap. They think they make themselves look good by taking credit, but what that shows to ***their*** managers is a lack of noteworthy contributions by team overall, so really…how good of a manager could this person be if the team is not contributing. In the end, it is far better to, as the old saying goes, give credit where credit is due. I would even go beyond that and advise to occasionally give credit sometimes even when or where it's not due. As a Manager, I ensure my teams always receive the credit and get the spotlight for the efforts that get noticed, even if it was entirely my own effort. Why? Well, as mentioned before, a job of a manager is to train the team so if my team is getting credit that reflects positively on me as a manager. It also ensures the team itself remains motivated. And truthfully, I may have felt I'd done 100% of the work, but in reality that would not be possible if my team wasn't good enough to back me up.

Acts of unselfishness abound in military history, from the guy jumping on a grenade to save his friends, to the Navy Corpsman braving withering gunfire to treat a wounded Marine. There is no shortage of unselfish acts to be found in combat – often tied very, very closely to Courage (discussed later).

It is worthwhile to note that it seems that the Marine Corps leadership in this area is a bit different from the other armed services – the Marine's at the highest level are always quick to give full credit to the Marines in their command rather than taking the glory and credit themselves – this is why you see so many heroic stories of enlisted men and lower ranking officers rather than having well known General grade officers. We all know who General Patton was, we all know who Admiral Nimitz was, but who was General Yates? General Yates was one of the Marine Generals in command during the battle of Iwo Jima, yet you've probably never heard of him. He eventually became the 19th Commandant of the Marine Corps. He was such a "Marine's Marine" that when his term of Commandant was over, he was voluntarily demoted from a four-star General to a three-star General so he could remain in the Marine Corps – that's quite an act of unselfishness in itself.

In the Corporate world, where real bullets are not flying and real grenades are not about to explode, finding these unselfish acts is a bit more difficult. When moving up the corporate ladder can be based on miniscule accomplishments, managers are often tempted to take credit over their subordinates or peers. This would never cross the mind of an unselfish and professional manager.

Zig Ziglar is a one of the most popular public speakers in the world, commanding huge audiences wherever he appears. He is often hired for speaking engagements by companies looking to improve the performance of it's sales force. Ziglar has affected millions of people the world over, and one of his primary underlying messages is "You can have everything you want in life if you help enough other people get what they want". How's that for unselfishness?

If you need further assistance with the trait of Unselfishness, we can turn to the person who is probably the most recognized example in the entire world – Mother Theresa. Below are her words:

> People are often unreasonable, illogical, and self-centered; forgive them anyway.
> If you are kind, People may accuse you of selfish, ulterior motives; Be kind anyway.
> If you are successful, you will win some false friends and some true enemies; Succeed anyway.
> If you are honest and frank, people may cheat you; Be honest and frank anyway.
> What you spend years building, someone could destroy overnight; Build anyway.
> If you find serenity and happiness, there may be jealousy; Be happy anyway.
> The good you do today, people will often forget tomorrow; Do good anyway.
> Give the world the best you have, and it may never be enough; Give the world the best you've got anyway

Can you achieve this type of Unselfish mindset?

Action Items:

I can't think of any stronger Action items than expressed by Mother Theresa's words above – give them a shot and see how you feel at the outcome. This would even be a good effort to monitor on a daily basis to see how you match up to her words. Make a chart, keep track, hold yourself accountable.

~~

Courage

Dictionary Definition:
A quality of spirit that enables you to face danger of pain without showing

USMC Definition:
The mental quality that recognizes fear of danger or criticism, but enables a man to proceed in the face of it with calmness and firmness

Courage is the most important of all the virtues, because without courage you can't practice any other virtue consistently. You can practice any virtue erratically, but nothing consistently without courage.
Maya Angelou

One man with courage is a majority.
Thomas Jefferson

Any intelligent fool can make things bigger and more complex... It takes a touch of genius - and a lot of courage to move in the opposite direction.
Albert Einstein

Taught to push through fear, Marines develop many forms of courage. Physical courage allows them to face circumstances head on when others would run away. Moral courage allows them to do the right thing when others wouldn't.

Simply put, "courage" is the trait that allows you to look at a situation that causes you to be apprehensive, nervous or just downright fearful, and do what needs to be done anyway. It's natural to equate courage with battlefield actions, and rightly so, but courage applies equally to non-life threatening situations as well.

It's not hard to find examples of great courage in Marine Corps history – they are plentiful and exciting to read. It is difficult, however, to find a more courageous example in Marine Corps history than John Bradley – and he wasn't even a Marine. Attached to a Marine Corps unit, John Bradley survived the battle of Iwo Jima and earned the Navy Cross – the nation's second highest award for bravery. He earned this award for crawling to the aid of a wounded Marine and shielding him with his own body from enemy fire while hanging a bag of blood plasma on an upturned rifle. While waving away others who were trying to assist, he then dragged the wounded Marine 30 yards through enemy fire to safety. All of this happened after "Doc" found himself at the top of Mount Suribachi and was a participant in the famous Iwo Jima Flag Raising which has become a symbol of Marine Corps grit and tenacity. Many years later, after John Bradley died his family found out he had received the Navy Cross – he never told them nor did he talk about the battle itself. It's been said of the battle for Iwo Jima that it was "America's Battle" – a battle that had more casualties in one day than the battle for Guadalcanal had in two and a half months – the beaches at Normandy were safe and secure in 24 hours, but at Iwo Jima our boys fought and died for two weeks – one Marine died every 2 seconds at Iwo Jima, for 2 weeks. Just surviving the battle took unimaginable courage.

Like most traits, the more you're exposed to situations where it's needed and used, the more evolved your courage will become. Eleanor Roosevelt said, "Do one thing every day that scares you". Why? Because the more you do, the more comfortable you become with those feelings. The more comfortable you are with them, the more competent you'll become at overcoming them. The fear may still remain, but you learn to put it aside and act anyway.

Action Items:
    Away from the battlefield, in your office or wherever you find yourself working, courage will manifest itself in several ways:
    Your ability to stand up to your boss for what you believe is right.

    This could be asking for a raise, or it could be positioning yourself as an advocate for a given policy or even an attempt at superior customer support.

Every company in the known galaxy today claims "superior customer service" and usually also claims to have an environment that "empowers" their workers to make tough decisions. In reality, many companies offer simply terrible customer service and if you work for one of these companies and are in a position to actually make positive changes, you'll have to get over your fear of failure, fear of embarrassment, fear of confrontation and fear of *fill-in-the-blank* and approach your boss with your recommendations.

In your personal life, you are faced with situations that require courage to see them through. Not "battlefield" courage, or even "office" courage but more of an emotional and personal courage.

Face new situations squarely with the knowledge that you may not be 100% successful, but you will survive and be stronger – and the next time you'll be even better.

Public speaking comes to mind here. Popular studies show that generally, people fear public speaking more than they fear death. However, as a person who once trembled at a podium and couldn't form a single sentence…and sat down a miserable mass of failure incarnate, I can tell you that once again, the more you do it, the better you become. I now love speaking and teaching and when given the opportunity to do so, always take advantage of it. In fact, it's tough to get me off the stage once I get started.

~~

Knowledge

Dictionary Definition: The psychological result of perception and learning and reasoning

USMC Definition: Understanding of a science or an art. The range of one's information, including professional knowledge and an understanding of your Marines

I was bold in the pursuit of knowledge, never fearing to follow truth and reason to whatever results they led, and bearding every authority which stood in their way.
Thomas Jefferson

An investment in knowledge pays the best interest.
Benjamin Franklin

Knowledge has to be improved, challenged, and increased constantly, or it vanishes.
Peter Drucker

A constant push at self-improvement ensures Marines are always learning. The ability to make sound judgment calls and accurate decisions are based on what they have learned either through study or experience – or both.

The concept of "knowledge" is far reaching – it affects every aspect of a Marine's job. There is no position that doesn't require knowledge to perform well, and the more knowledge obtained, the better the job will be performed. Marines are expected to know not only their job, but also the jobs and responsibilities of those around and above them. To be effective in combat, a unit must be able to survive the loss of key people and the best way to ensure this is to ensure everybody understands everybody else's job. As you can imagine, this takes a lot of work, a lot of study, and a lot of effort.

A perfect example of a Marine who took "knowledge" very seriously was Carlos Hathcock – one of the deadliest snipers in Marine Corps history (currently ranks 3rd in the Marine Corps in confirmed kills). In Vietnam, because of his extremely high count of confirmed kills, the NVA put a bounty of $30,000 on his head – most US snipers rated a bounty between $8-$30. By the end of his time in Vietnam, he had been credited with 93 confirmed kills.

Why would knowledge be important for a sniper? Weapon knowledge, terrain knowledge, survival knowledge, troop movement knowledge, even a bit of philosophical and physiological understanding of his opponents was required.

> Hathcock knew his weapons well – he knew what to expect of them, he knew their limitations, he knew how to best deploy himself and his weapons to gain the most advantage.
> Hathcock understood the terrain and how it could be used to his advantage. He also understood the importance of escape routes to ensure he did not get boxed in once the bullets started flying.
> Usually, snipers will travel with a spotter and that's about it. Two people, alone for long durations in unfriendly territory requires in depth knowledge of how to survive off the land.
> Hathcock studied and understood how his targets moved and what their tendencies were. Knowing this enabled him to put himself in the best position for a successful result.

Most of the times a sniper is after a single target and can then disappear. Sometimes a sniper is called to pin down an entire unit. Understanding how the enemy will react once they are attacked ensures the best positioning as well as the best egress route.

Two interesting sidebars about Carlos Hathcock – neither of which have anything to do with "Knowledge", but certainly brings into play the other traits we are discussing.

He normally wore a white feather in his bush hat – it was his trademark so to speak and the Viet Cong called him Long Trang which translates as "White Feather". Only one time did he remove the feature from his hat – when he took out an NVA General. Crawling inch by inch for 1500 yards, it took him four days to get into position. During these four days of no sleep, he was almost stepped on by the enemy patrols and at one point was almost bitten by a viper. Regardless of this, he got his shot, the General died, and then then had to crawl back the way he came. An amazing feat.

The Viet Cong dispatched a platoon of highly trained snipers to hunt down the American sniper with the white feather – when this became known many Marines operating in the same area took it upon themselves to wear white feathers to confuse the enemy snipers. These Marines realized how valuable Hathcock's efforts were and took it upon themselves to put themselves in danger to help ensure Hathcock remained a threat.

Action Items:

First, don't go out and buy a sniper rifle…please.

Work to fully understand your role where you work. Once you have full understanding you are in a good position to identify your knowledge deficiencies and take corrective action

It's a pretty well-worn statement to urge you to specialization rather than generalization. Not to be cliché, but I do agree with that advice for the most part. Generalization will get your foot in the door but won't command as high of a salary as specialization. You can specialize, and still maintain a well-rounded generalization as well.

~~

Loyalty

Dictionary Definition: The act of binding yourself (intellectually or emotionally) to a course of action

USMC Definition: The quality of faithfulness to country, the Corps, the unit, to one's seniors, subordinates and peers

I'll take fifty percent efficiency to get one hundred percent loyalty.
Samuel Goldwyn

Success is the result of perfection, hard work, learning from failure, loyalty, and persistence.
Colin Powell

The thing I was attracted to as a little girl was Kirk, Bones and Spock, and their utter loyalty. There's nothing more powerful than that.
Jolene Blalock

A Marine's loyalty to his fellow Marines, the Corps and the United States is deeply entrenched. The Motto we are taught on the first day of boot camp, Semper Fidelis, means "Always Faithful", representing the loyalty Marines have for the Marines they fight alongside of as well as the communities they belong to.

Loyalty in the military comes in many flavors – the most common exists in the relationship between a leader and her or her subordinates. We've all seen the war movies where the unlikeable and inept platoon commander, usually a young lieutenant, has not earned the respect or loyalty of his troops and ends up either getting "fragged" with a grenade or shot by his own troops. This is an obvious case where loyalty was lacking. In combat, nobody wants to be led by an incompetent leader as that's how entire units get wiped out…much better to take a poor leader out of the picture then to let that leader get an entire unit killed. Sounds violent and maybe a little over the edge, but for the young troops that are supposed throw their lives away, it's easy math.

The Marine Corps Motto is "Semper Fidelis", which means "Always Faithful". This statement is the embodiment of loyalty – loyalty to "God, Country and Corps". Marines are taught and reinforced throughout their time in the Corps that loyalty is critical to maintain the other traits. Without loyalty, integrity, dependability, bearing, judgment and the others all go out the window. Compromise your loyalty one time and it can take a lifetime to earn it back, if even then.

In the corporate world, Loyalty is on display on a daily basis. How you back your team and your team members, how you talk about the company you work for, how you talk to your peers about management and how you talk to management about your peers. All of this is based on your loyalty.

Loyalty works up and down the organization. You must be loyal to your peers, your subordinates, your management and your company.

Action Items:
> Defend your employer. These days it's almost a rite of passage to complain about your employer or your boss or your manager. Don't participate in this – rather take up a defense and ensure others realize you are loyal to those who employ you. As Elbert Hubbard said, "If you work for a man, in heaven's name, work for him: Speak well of him and stand by the institution he represents. Remember, an ounce of loyalty is worth a pound of cleverness. If you must growl, condemn, and eternally find fault, resign your position and when you are on the outside, complain to your heart's content." The gist is simply to not bite the hand that feeds you. Doing otherwise degrades you and your reputation.
>
> Look for extreme signs of loyalty around you and understand why they are noteworthy. This can in a corporate setting, on the news, on a TV show (as mentioned in the quote above about Star Trek) or anywhere else. Work to understand where the loyalties lie, why they are so strong, how they were built, etc. When you understand this, you are much better positioned to both earn and give loyalty.

~

Endurance
Dictionary Definition: The power to withstand hardship or stress

USMC Definition: The mental and physical stamina measured by the ability to withstand pain, fatigue, stress and hardship

Come what may, all bad fortune is to be conquered by endurance.
Virgil

Endurance is not just the ability to bear a hard thing, but to turn it into glory.
William Barclay

The men who learn endurance, are they who call the whole world, brother.
Charles Dickens

It's impossible to lead from the front if you're falling behind. Every Marine is expected to be a leader, and therefore have the endurance to do so in any circumstance. Marines continue on when others quit, always giving more than most think is possible. Endurance is an individual effort and trait, but it's also the ability to convince others that they too can go the extra mile.

Once again, we turn to the Korean War, on the frozen terrain of the Chosin Resevoir for a perfect example of not only Endurance but just about every other positive attribute you can think of. I'll include this Marine's entire Medal of Honor citation below. I usually like to discuss the younger Marine's efforts, but the citation below is for a Lt. Col – one of the "older" Marines. In addition to what is displayed below, this Marine also fought in World War II and Vietnam, earning a Navy Cross, two Distinguished Service Medals, two Silver Stars, and many other awards. He served for over three decades, commanding every level of combat from Platoon to Division. He fought in fourteen campaigns and has been awarded seven Foreign Awards. Here's his Medal of Honor citation:

For conspicuous gallantry and intrepidity at the risk of his life above and beyond the call of duty as Commanding Officer of the First Battalion, Seventh Marines, First Marine Division (Reinforced), in aware that the operation involved breaking through a surrounding enemy and advancing eight miles along primitive icy trails in the bitter cold with every passage disputed by a savage and determined foe, Lieutenant Colonel Davis boldly led his battalion into the attack in a daring attempt to relieve a beleaguered rifle company and to seize, hold and defend a vital mountain pass controlling the only route available for two Marine regiments in danger of being cut off by numerically superior hostile force during their redeployment to the port of Hungnam. When the battalion immediately encountered strong opposition from entrenched enemy forces commanding high ground in the path of the advance, he promptly spearheaded his unit in a fierce attack up the steep, ice-covered slopes in the face of withering fire and, personally leading the assault groups in a hand-to-hand encounter, drove the hostile troops from their positions, rested his mean and reconnoitered the area under enemy fire to determine the best route for continuing the mission. Always in the thick of fighting, Lieutenant Colonel Davis let his battalion over three successive ridges in the deep snow in continuous attacks against the enemy and, constantly inspiring and encouraging his men throughout the night, brought his unit to a point within 1500 yards of the surrounded rifle company by daybreak. Although knocked to the ground when a shell fragment struck his helmet and two bullets pierced this clothing, he arose and fought his way forward at the head of his men until he reached the isolated Marines. On the following morning, he bravely led his battalion in securing the vital mountain pass from a strongly entrenched and numerically superior hostile force, carrying all his wounded with him, including 22 litter cases and held the vital terrain until the two regiments of the division had deployed through the pass and, on the morning of 4 December, led his battalion into Hagaru-ri intact. By his superb leadership, outstanding courage and brilliant tactical ability, Lieutenant Colonel Davis was directly instrumental in saving the beleaguered rifle company from complete annihilation and enabled the two Marine regiments to escape possible destruction. His valiant devotion to duty and unyielding fighting spirit in the face of almost insurmountable odds enhance and sustain the highest traditions of the United States Naval Service.

I get tired just reading about what Lt. Col Davis did – simply amazing. Obviously he was a man with great endurance. Physical endurance allowed him to run all over the battlefield to achieve his mission and protect his Marines, it allowed him to fight in three wars, it allowed him to hold more commands than most military officers could dream of. All of this takes a large amount of mental or emotional endurance as well. You can imagine the numbers of his troops he saw fall in battle over the years, the constant concern for the safety of his troops, a commitment to "get the job done" while at the same time doing his best to allow his Marines to get back home when it was all over. Doing that for over 30 years is bound to be emotionally taxing as well – so emotional Endurance is every bit as important as physical Endurance. In fact, it can be argued it is more important – for many, the act of "giving up" starts in their minds and works its way into their actions.

Physical Endurance in the corporate world can be of critical importance at times, but I would wager that emotional endurance is key. In most corporate jobs, you aren't tasked with physically demanding jobs, but rather emotionally draining ones.

Bear in mind that developing your endurance means more than just being able to "take it", you must be able to take it, and still perform at your peak. It's one thing to get to the end of the day or week and have nothing left – it's quite another to get to the end of the day or week and still be ready to put in more hours if they are called for. There is no overtime for salaried employees – you're expected to work until the job is done. If that takes you past the 10-12 hour day or the 50-60 hour week, your mind and your body must be able to not only get through it, but should be able to go the extra mile when needed.

Action Items:
    Work on your physical endurance. Every task you undertake in your entire life will be easier and have a much high probability of success if you have the physical endurance to push through it.

    Work on your mental endurance. Even more than physical endurance, your mental state will determine how much you can handle.

    Think back to the last effort you attempted and did not finish – was endurance (physical or mental) a cause for the failure? What could have been done differently?

~

Extra Credit

I hope you have found this information both entertaining and useful. When my writings have anything to do with the Marine Corps, I sometimes tend to go overboard as my beloved Corps is still so much a part of my life and lifestyle, I tend to get carried away. From the stories you've read, hopefully have a strong respect for Marine Corps leadership, and therefore a strong value for the Leadership Traits that have made the Marine Corps what it is today and has been for over 200 years.

I would encourage further research if you find the information in this book useful. There are plenty of sites that outline these Traits as well as other Leadership based philosophies. I'll end this book with a bit more of Marine Corps Leadership thoughts – outline the Leadership Principles.

    Know yourself and seek self-improvement.
    Be technically and tactically proficient.

Develop a sense of responsibility among your subordinates.

Make sound and timely decisions.

Set the example.

Know your Marines and look out for their welfare.

Keep your Marines informed.

Seek responsibility and take responsibility for your actions.

Ensure assigned tasks are understood, supervised, and accomplished.

Train your Marines as a team.

Employ your command in accordance with its capabilities.

Semper Fi!

~~

Thank You!

I want to extend my most sincere thanks to you for buying and reading this book – and trusting me to provide something of value. I hope you have found at least a few nuggets within these pages that will enable you to further your endeavors and eclipse every goal you have set for yourself. I'm pretty busy, but never too busy to directly respond to a reader and potential friend so if you have the time I would consider it a huge honor if you would go to the $60K Jobs website (www.60KJobs.com) and subscribe, leaving me your email and maybe a short note. I promise a response and hopefully the beginning of a friendship as well.

~~

About the Author

Perry Hurtt was born in Hillsboro, Oregon in 1965. Joining the Marine Corps as soon as he graduated Lower Lake High School in 1983, he spent the next 16 years traveling the globe and working in many different capacities as the Marine Corps saw fit. In March of 2000, Perry was honorably discharged from the Marine Corps, having gained the rank of Gunnery Sergeant (E7) and went to work for Corporate America. Since 2000 Perry has worked for 3 different companies in numerous positions to fully apply the leadership traits learned in the Marine Corps.

While continuing the corporate drudgery, Perry has also created and is championing the concept of "$60K Jobs - the idea that a person can undertake certain occupations with no college and no experience and obtain a $5K per month income within 90 days, thereby achieving a $60K salary. See the website at www.60KJobs.com.

Happily married for over 25 years to Geni, he is also the proud father of his son Steven and daughter Angela. Geni and Perry live in Covington, Georgia and spend most of their free time caring for and rescuing stray dogs.

~~

Other Works
These works, and a lot of other material can be found at the $60K Jobs days website at http://www.60KJobs.com

$0 to $60K in 90 Days - Auto Sales - With no college degree or experience, increase your income to $5K per month after 90 days as an Auto Sales Professional

$0 to $60K in 90 Days - Bartender - With no college degree or experience, increase your income to $5K per month after 90 days as a Bartender

$0 to $60K in 90 Days - Unix Administrator - With no college degree or experience, increase your income to $5K per month after 90 days as a Unix Administrator

Back To Top

Made in the
USA
Middletown, DE